5 STEP ENGLISH
Cinderella

5단계로 술술 읽히는 영어원서
단계 영어 신데렐라

초   판 | 1쇄 발행 2025년 10월 20일

지 은 이 | 샤를페로
영어번역 | 신자경, 스티브오
그   림 | M.J 화이트
정보맵핑 | 이야기 연구소
디 자 인 | 박소영
제 작 처 | 다온피앤피
특허등록 | 10-2717987호
국제출원 | PCT/KE202/002551

펴 낸 곳 | ㈜도서출판동행
펴 낸 이 | 오승근
출판등록 | 2020년 3월 20일 제2020-000005호
주   소 | 부산광역시 부산진구 동천로 109, 9층
이 메 일 | withyou@withyoubooks.com
카카오톡 | @도서출판동행

단계별 요약정보 기술은 국내특허등록 및 PCT 국제출원을 했습니다.

이 책은 저작권법에 따라 보호받는 저작물이므로 무단 전재와 복제를 금지하며,
이 책 내용의 전부 또는 일부를 이용하려면 반드시 출판사의 서면 동의를 받아야 합니다.
잘못된 책은 구입하신 서점에서 바꿔 드립니다.

ISBN 979-11-91648-50-8 (13740)

5단계로 **술술 읽히는** 영어원서

단계영어

신데렐라

머리말
Prologue

언어 실력이 자라날수록,
영어책도 함께 자라야 합니다.

아이에게 신발이나 옷을 사줄 때 한 치수 크게 고르는 이유가 뭘까요? 바로 아이가 빠르게 자라기 때문입니다. 사실 아이의 신체만큼이나 머릿속 사고력도 금방 자라납니다. 그리고 사고력이 자랄수록, 아이가 접하는 영어책도 함께 '성장'해야 합니다.

어린 나뭇가지를 그냥 두면 제멋대로 휘어 자라지만, 어릴 때 곧은 부목으로 지지해주면 올곧게 자라는 것처럼, 아이의 학습도 비슷합니다. 매번 나무를 뽑고 더 큰 나무를 새로 심기보다는, 하나의 나무를 끝까지 가꾸는 법을 알려주는 편이 훨씬 좋습니다. 이 책도 같은 맥락에서 시작되었습니다. **하나의 스토리를 아이 수준에 맞춰 5단계로 발전시키는 신개념 영어 도서이니까요.**

아이들이 말을 배워가는 과정을 떠올려보세요. 처음에는 "엄마", "아빠"처럼 단 몇 단어만 말하지만, 시간이 흐를수록 말이 길어지고 내용도 깊어집니다. 예를 들어, 처음엔 "엄마 밥 줘"라고 말하던 아이가 나중에는 "엄마, 내가 좋아하는 김밥 먹고 싶어요"라고 표현하게 되죠. 중요한 것은 표현이 달라져도 "배가 고파서 음식을 먹고 싶다"는 핵심은 같다는 사실입니다.

이 책의 5단계 영어 구성은 바로 이런 언어 발달 과정을 그대로 담았습니다. 예를 들어, 레벨 1은 네 살 아이의 표현, 레벨 2는 다섯 살 아이의 표현과 비슷하다고 볼 수 있습니다. **전하고자 하는 메시지는 같지만, 표현 방식은 점점 더 풍부해지는 것이죠.**

계단을 오르듯이 레벨별로 차근차근 읽어보세요. 아이의 사고력과 함께 영어 실력도 자연스럽게 자라날 것입니다.

스티브 오

When you buy shoes or clothes for your child, you often choose a size up because you know they're going to grow. Children's thoughts expand just as quickly, so it makes sense for their English books to evolve as well.

If young twigs aren't supported, they'll grow bent and crooked. However, if you straighten a branch that has fallen to the ground by tying it to a sturdy splint, it will grow upright. Children are no different. Instead of uprooting a sapling to plant a bigger one, teach them to care for the tree they have. This book presents a new approach: it unfolds a story in five stages tailored to different reading levels.

Think about how children learn to speak. A child who can only say "mom" or "dad" soon starts to form longer words and more meaningful sentences. They might first say, "Give me food, Mom," but later, that evolves into something like "Mom, I want to eat my favorite food, gimbap." Even though the words change, the intention—"I'm hungry" or "I want to eat"—remains the same.

In 5 Step English, the natural course of a child's language development—what usually takes three to four years—has been divided into five levels. Level 1 reflects the way a typical four-year-old might speak; Level 2 matches a five-year-old, and so on. The core idea stays consistent, but the complexity of the expression increases with each level.

I encourage you to read through each level as though you're climbing a set of steps, one at a time.

Steve Oh

사용설명서
Manual

단계 영어
오디오북 채널

영어는 언어입니다. 영어는 암기보단, **실제 사용을 통해 익혀야 합니다.** 즉, 의미가 있어야 하고 내가 사용해야 합니다. 이 책은 학습자가 아닌 책으로서 영어를 의미있게 사용할 수 있게 제작했습니다.

간단하지만 명확하게 도서 사용방법을 말씀드리겠습니다.

❶ 영어 공부가 아닌 **책을 읽는다고 생각하세요.**

❷ **레벨 1부터 읽으세요.** 레벨1이 무척 쉽게보여도 일단 레벨 1부터 읽어야 다음 단계로 수월하게 올라갈 수 있습니다. 마치 계단을 오를 때, 첫 계단에 발을 내디디고 그 다음 계단으로 오르는 것처럼 말입니다.

❸ 모르는 단어가 보이면 **사전을 찾지 마세요.** 다시 한번 말씀드리지만 이건 책입니다. 책은 읽어야 합니다. 우리가 보통 책을 읽을 때 국어사전을 찾으면서 읽지않는 것처럼 말입니다.

❹ **레벨 5까지 읽었다면 이제 레벨 4, 3 순으로 거꾸로 읽어보세요.** 복잡한 문장들이 어떻게 간략하게 요약되는지를 배울 수 있게 됩니다.

사용법은 위 4가지면 충분합니다.

자, 그럼 이제 시작해 볼까요?

---

1) 레벨5에서는 사전을 찾으셔도 됩니다. 내용 이해를 위해서가 아닌 모르는 단어의 정확한 의미 파악을 위해 사전을 찾을 필요가 있습니다.

Audio Book
Channel

English is a language, Language should be learned through practical use rather than memorization. That means, it has to make sense and you have to use it. This book is not a study book, but a book designed to use English in a meaningful way.

I will tell you how to use the book in a simple but clear way.

❶ Do not think that you study English. Instead, read the book.

❷ Read the book from level 1. Even if level 1 looks very easy, you should read level 1 first to move up to the next level with ease. It's just like climbing the stairs. When you go upstairs, you place your foot on the first stair and then go up to the next one.

❸ If you see word you don't know, don't consult a Dictionary. a Again, this is a book. The book must be read. It's just like we don't consult an English dictionary when we usually read an English book.

❹ If you have read all the way to level 5, now read books backwards in order of level 4 and 3. You will learn how to concisely summarize complex sentences.

If you have learned above 4 methods, it is sufficient.

So, let's get started, shall we?

목 차
Contents

단계 영어
오디오북 채널

머리말

독자 후기

도서 사용법

Cinderella **LEVEL 1**   14

Chapter 1 The Fireplace Maid	16
Chapter 2 The Fairy's Gift	20
Chapter 3 The First Ball	28
Chapter 4 The Second Ball	32
Chapter 5 The Midnight Escape	38
Chapter 6 The Glass Slipper	44

Cinderella **LEVEL 2**   50

Chapter 1 The Fireplace Maid	52
Chapter 2 The Fairy's Gift	56
Chapter 3 The First Ball	62
Chapter 4 The Second Ball	66
Chapter 5 The Midnight Escape	72
Chapter 6 The Glass Slipper	76

Cinderella **LEVEL 3**   82

Chapter 1 The Fireplace Maid	84
Chapter 2 The Fairy's Gift	88
Chapter 3 The First Ball	96
Chapter 4 The Second Ball	100
Chapter 5 The Midnight Escape	106
Chapter 6 The Glass Slipper	112

Cinderella **LEVEL 4**   116

Chapter 1 The Fireplace Maid	118
Chapter 2 The Fairy's Gift	122
Chapter 3 The First Ball	128
Chapter 4 The Second Ball	132
Chapter 5 The Midnight Escape	136
Chapter 6 The Glass Slipper	140

Cinderella **LEVEL 5**   144

Chapter 1 The Fireplace Maid	146
Chapter 2 The Fairy's Gift	150
Chapter 3 The First Ball	156
Chapter 4 The Second Ball	160
Chapter 5 The Midnight Escape	164
Chapter 6 The Glass Slipper	168

단계영어

· 신데렐라 ·

LEVEL 1

단어(Words)

1193개

LOW　　　　　　　MIDDLE　　　　　　　HIGH

문장수(Sentences)

159개

LOW　　　　　　　MIDDLE　　　　　　　HIGH

문장길이(Sentence Length)

7.5

LOW　　　　　　　MIDDLE　　　　　　　HIGH

읽는 시간(Reading time)

4분 46초

LOW　　　　　　　MIDDLE　　　　　　　HIGH

말하는 시간(Speaking Time)

9분 10초

LOW　　　　　　　MIDDLE　　　　　　　HIGH

Chapter 1
The Fireplace Maid

Ella was a pretty girl. Everyone liked her. Ella's mother had died.

Ella got a new mother and new sisters. Her new mother loved only her daughters.

Ella worked hard, but they did not. They called her Cinderella.

The King and Queen had a son. They wanted him to get married. They invited all the ladies to a party.

Cinderella's new mother and sisters received invitations too. They were excited.

The sisters wanted the Prince. He was kind and nice. Every lady liked him. The sisters got nice dresses and beautiful things.

Cinderella sighed, "I want to go to the party." The new mother and sisters laughed at her. "Go wash the dishes!" they ordered. Cinderella worked in the kitchen, and she cried and cried.

Chapter 2
The Fairy's Gift

The sisters wore pretty dresses. They showed them to Cinderella. Cinderella felt a little sad.

The sisters and new mother got on a cart. They went to the party. Cinderella sat near the fire and cried a bit.

Suddenly, an old woman appeared in the kitchen. "Why

are you sad, dear?" she asked. Cinderella replied, "I wanted to go to the party, but only my sisters went."

"Don't cry," said the old woman. "I'll help you. You can go to the party. Go to the garden and find six friendly mice and a pumpkin."

In a small cage in the garden, Cinderella found six mice. She also found a big pumpkin. She brought both the pumpkin and the six mice. Then she also gave the old woman a rat.

"Great," said the old woman. Using her magic wand, she turned the pumpkin into a large cart and the six mice into six horses. The rat became the driver. He hopped onto the cart and waited.

"Helpers! Helpers!" the old woman called. She had no helpers, so she found two lizards and turned them into helpers.

"All set!" she said. "My clothes!" Cinderella worried. The old woman changed Cinderella's clothes into a beautiful blue dress that shone brilliantly.

Cinderella was very happy. The old woman said, "Remember this: you must be home by midnight. Everything will change at twelve o'clock." Cinderella promised.

Chapter 3
The First Ball

Cinderella went to the big castle. Inside, there was the Prince and many ladies. Everyone wanted the Prince.

Cinderella walked into the room. Many people saw her, including the Prince. She was very, very pretty.

He chose her and said, "You're so beautiful. Can you dance

with me?" So the Prince and Cinderella danced together. The Prince liked Cinderella a lot and asked her name, but she didn't tell him.

At 11:45, she suddenly left the party and went outside. She was gone.

Cinderella came back home, and everything changed back. Soon, her sisters arrived. "Was the party nice? Who danced with the Prince?" Cinderella asked. "A special princess," her sisters replied. "No one knew who she was, and no one could find her. She suddenly left before twelve. There's another party tomorrow night. The Prince will find her."

Cinderella felt sad. "I want to go too," she said. "Oh no, it's not for you," her sisters said. "You must stay in the kitchen." They went to bed early for the party.

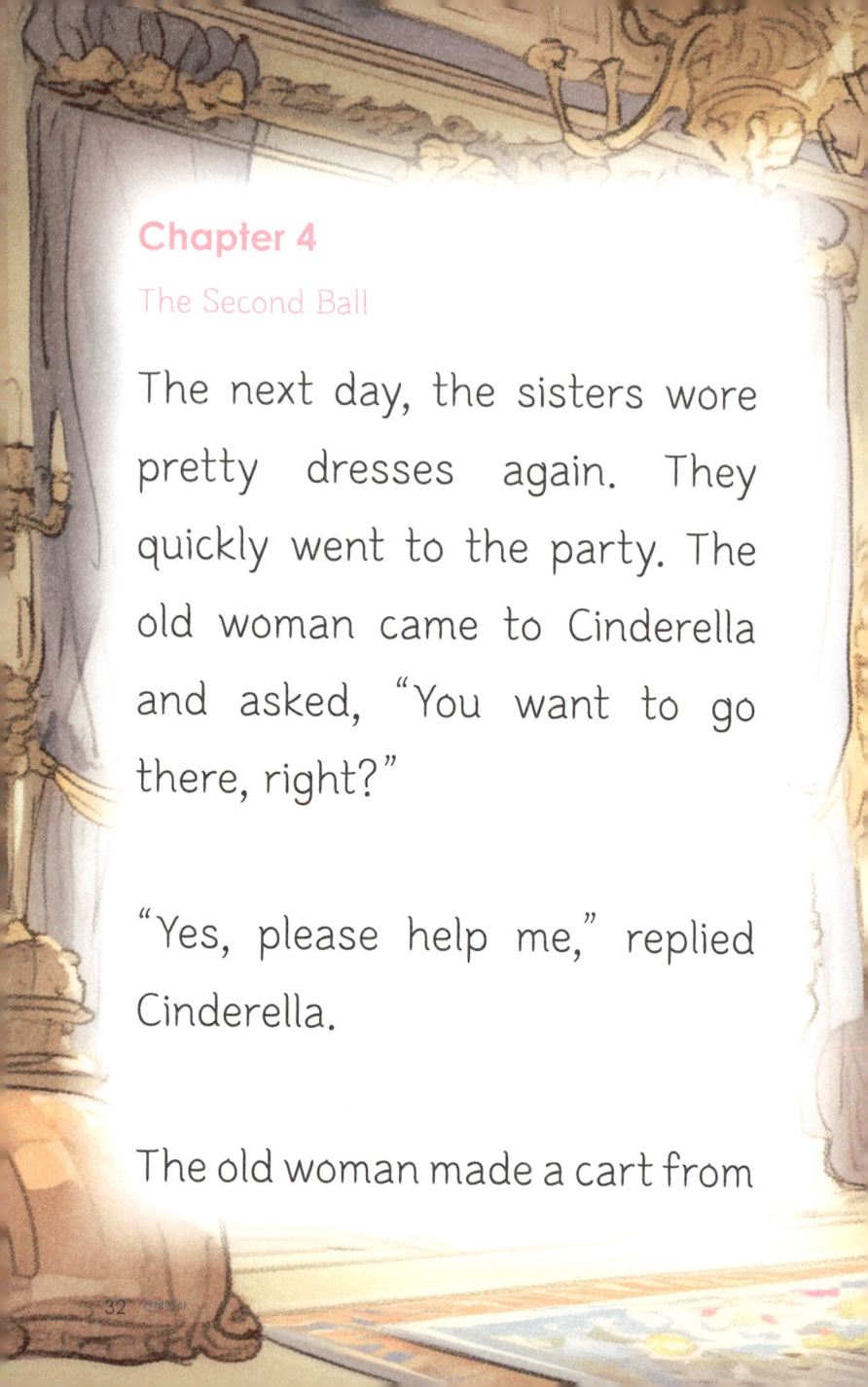

Chapter 4
The Second Ball

The next day, the sisters wore pretty dresses again. They quickly went to the party. The old woman came to Cinderella and asked, "You want to go there, right?"

"Yes, please help me," replied Cinderella.

The old woman made a cart from

a pumpkin. She turned mice into horses, a rat into a driver, and lizards into helpers. Then she helped Cinderella put on a beautiful dress. Now Cinderella could go to the party.

The Prince was waiting for Cinderella. He was happy to see her. He held her hand and asked, "Where did you go last night? I looked everywhere." They danced together again. But

Cinderella had to leave before twelve.

Finally, she started to run away. She jumped into the cart, and soon it turned back into a pumpkin near her house. The horses turned back into mice, and the driver became a rat. Her dress became her old clothes again. She sat by the fire in the kitchen until her sisters returned.

"Wow, it was a great party!" her sisters shouted. "The Princess was the most beautiful. The Prince only looked at her and liked her a lot." Hearing this, Cinderella felt sad.

"Come here! Help us take off our dresses. We're going to the party again tomorrow. We need to go to bed now," they said. Cinderella helped her sisters, and they talked about the Prince and Princess.

Chapter 5

The Midnight Escape

The next night arrived. Her sisters dressed up for the party and went without her.

Then, the old woman appeared again and asked, "Do you want to go too?"

"Of course, I do. I really want to," said Cinderella.

"Okay, you can go, but you must leave before twelve. Everything will change back again, okay?" replied the old woman.

Cinderella promised, and the old woman used her magic. She made a new dress for her. Cinderella wore it and went to the party.

She arrived safely at the party. Everyone was dancing. She saw the Prince again, and he was very happy to see her. They danced together many times.

Cinderella was very happy. But then it turned twelve. The clock went "ding-dong"! Cinderella was surprised and started running away.

She hurried down the stairs and accidentally left behind her shiny shoe. The ringing stopped, and everything turned back. Her dress became her old clothes, and she felt sad.

Cinderella ran home quickly. "Why are you so sad?" her sisters asked. "Wow, the Princess was so pretty today. The Prince only looked at her, but she left again!"

The Prince found her shoe on the stairs. Maybe he can find her using it. Oh, I want to be her," they said.

Chapter 6
The Glass Slipper

The next day, the Prince said to everyone, "I found her shoe! I'll find my princess with it."

The Prince really wanted to find her. People took it to different houses. All the ladies tried it on, but it didn't fit anyone. Some feet were too long, others too big, and some too small.

Finally, someone came to Cinderella's house. Her sisters were very excited. They tried on the special shoe, but it didn't fit their feet.

The mother told them to try again, but the man said, "Is there anyone else in this house?"

The mother replied, "We have a little kitchen maid, but she stayed at home. She didn't go to the party." Nevertheless, the man wanted to see her.

So, the mother called Cinderella, and she came quickly. She looked so pretty and nice.

Cinderella took the shoe from the man and put it on—it fit perfectly.

He said, "Now you are my princess!" Then, the mother

and sisters became very angry. They couldn't believe it.

After that, the man took her to the Prince. The Prince missed her so much, so he was very happy. She wore a beautiful dress. She looked so beautiful. They got married and were happy together forever.

단계영어

신데렐라

LEVEL 2

단어(Words)
1367개 — LOW · MIDDLE · HIGH

문장수(Sentences)
170개 — LOW · MIDDLE · HIGH

문장길이(Sentence Length)
8 — LOW · MIDDLE · HIGH

읽는 시간(Reading time)
5분 28초 — LOW · MIDDLE · HIGH

말하는 시간(Speaking Time)
10분 30초 — LOW · MIDDLE · HIGH

Chapter 1
The Fireplace Maid

Cinderella was a kind and beautiful girl. Everyone loved her. One day, her mother passed away.

After that, she had a new mother and new sisters. But her new mother only gave good things to her own daughters.

They had nice clothes, but Cinderella

had old ones. She worked hard, while her sisters did nothing.

There was a King and Queen. They had only one son, and they wanted him to find a princess. So, they invited all the ladies to a party. Cinderella's new mother and sisters were invited too. They were really excited. All of them wanted the Prince because he was gentle and kind.

The sisters got beautiful clothes. They had shiny jewels, fancy hairpins, and pretty fans. The new mother had lovely clothes, too.

Cinderella sighed, "I want to go to the party, too. I want to see the Prince." But her new mother and sisters just laughed. "Just go wash the dishes!" So Cinderella worked and felt sad.

Chapter 2
The Fairy's Gift

The sisters wore wonderful dresses. They went to the kitchen and showed their dresses to Cinderella. She was jealous of her sisters. Her new sisters and mother got on the horse cart.

They went to the party without Cinderella. After that, Cinderella sat by the fire and cried a lot.

Suddenly, an old woman appeared in front of her. Cinderella did not know

her. The old woman asked, "Why are you so sad, my dear?" Cinderella looked at her. "I wanted to go to the party. I am sad because only my sisters went there."

"Don't worry. Stop crying," said the woman. "I can help you. If you do as I say, you will have everything. First, go to the garden and bring me a pumpkin and six mice.

Cinderella found a big pumpkin and carried it, along with six mice and a rat.

"Good, now we are ready!" said the woman. Suddenly, the pumpkin turned into a great cart using her magic wand. She also turned six mice into six horses and the rat into a driver. He jumped onto the cart and waited.

Then the old woman said, "Helpers! Helpers!" She found two lizards and turned them into helpers.
"Everything is ready!" said the woman.

"Oh, my clothes!" cried Cinderella.

She was worried about her old clothes. "Wait!" The woman touched her clothes and changed them into a wonderful blue dress.

Cinderella loved it so much; she felt very happy. Her blue dress shone brightly.

"You must come home by 12 o'clock. Remember this: If you don't do that, everything will change back," the old woman said. Cinderella promised, and then she got on the cart.

Chapter 3
The First Ball

She arrived at the castle. The Prince and many ladies were enjoying the party. Just then, Cinderella entered the room. Everyone looked at her because she was so pretty.

The Prince chose her and held her hand, saying, "Will you be my partner? You are so beautiful."

They started dancing together. The Prince danced only with Cinderella.

He wanted to know her name, but she wouldn't tell him.

Before 12:00, she ran away quickly and nobody found her.

Cinderella came home and sat by the fire. Her dress turned old again. Her sisters also came home. "Was it good?" she asked.

"Yes, it was good," they replied. "Who was the Prince's partner?"

"The Prince danced with a mysterious princess. She suddenly disappeared, and he couldn't find her. He probably wants her to come to the party tomorrow."

Cinderella was really sad. "Please take me with you," she begged.

"What?" her sisters shouted. "What a shame! Stay in the kitchen. That is your place." They went to bed to prepare for the next party.

Chapter 4
The Second Ball

The next night, the sisters got ready and went to the party once more. Cinderella really wanted to go with them. Then, the old woman entered the kitchen and asked, "You want to go to party, right?"

Cinderella replied, "Of course, I do. I need your help."

The woman told her to bring a pumpkin, six mice, a rat, and lizards.

She turned them into a cart, horses, a driver, and helpers. Meanwhile, Cinderella's clothes turned into a wonderful dress, thanks to the magic wand. Cinderella got into the cart and went to the party.

Finally, she arrived and entered the room. The Prince saw her and held her hand, saying, "Where did you go? I looked for you everywhere. I missed you." They danced together, and he only had eyes for her.

It was almost twelve, and Cinderella felt nervous. She had to leave before twelve, but the Prince was watching her. She finally took a chance and ran quickly toward the door.

Soon, everything changed back. The cart turned into a pumpkin, the horses into mice, and the driver into a rat. Her beautiful dress also became old clothes again. She arrived home and sat beside the fire.

Her sisters returned and talked

loudly, "It was the best party ever! The princess was the most beautiful. The Prince watched only her and loved her." Cinderella listened and grew sad.

"Hey! Come and take off our dresses. We're going to another party tomorrow. We have to go to bed now," they shouted.

Cinderella helped the sisters, and they continued to talk about the beautiful princess and the handsome Prince.

Chapter 5
The Midnight Escape

The next day, Cinderella helped her sisters get dressed for the party. They left in a special cart.

Cinderella waited for the old woman, who soon arrived and asked, "Do you want to go to the party like them?"

Cinderella replied, "Yes, I really want to go there."

"Don't worry. I'll help you. But

remember, you must leave before twelve. Everything will change back at twelve," the woman cautioned.

Cinderella understood and promised to follow. The old woman then made a new dress for her using her wonderful magic.

Cinderella went to the party and people were dancing happily. The Prince and the mysterious Princess also danced together for a long time.

The Prince kept watching her as it became midnight. The clock rang loudly. Cinderella felt scared and ran away quickly.

Unfortunately, she left a glass shoe behind on the stairs and couldn't pick it up. She reached the door, and everything turned old; her shiny jewels disappeared, too. She cried a lot and hurried home.

Soon, her sisters returned and asked, "Why do you look sad? You don't have anything to worry about! Today, the princess was so beautiful. The Prince kept watching her, but she disappeared again! The Prince found only her glass shoe on the stairs. He may find her with it. Oh, I wish I could be her," they said.

Chapter 6
The Glass Slipper

The following morning, the Prince announced, "I found her shoe! I'm going to find the owner of it. She will be my princess." The mysterious girl had disappeared three times, but he decided to find her.

The Prince's helper took the shoe to every house. He gave every lady a chance to try it on. But it didn't fit anyone.

Eventually, the helper arrived at Cinderella's home. The sisters tried on the special shoe, but it didn't fit them either.

Their mother pushed them to try again. However, the helper said, "No one was the right one. Is there anyone else in this house?"

"Oh, we only have a little kitchen maid, but she isn't important. She was at home and didn't go to the party," the mother replied. Nonetheless, the helper wanted to see her. He had to check all the ladies.

The mother called for Cinderella, and she came right away. She looked very pretty and kind.

The helper thought, "Why didn't she go to the party?" Cinderella took the glass shoe from him and put it on; it fit her perfectly.

After that, the helper took her to the Prince in the palace. She wore a wonderful dress and looked like a princess at that party. The Prince was so happy to find her. They got married and lived together happily ever after.

단계영어

신데렐라

LEVEL 3

단어(Words)

1945개
LOW　　　　MIDDLE　　　　HIGH

문장수(Sentences)

190개
LOW　　　　MIDDLE　　　　HIGH

문장길이(Sentence Length)

10.2
LOW　　　　MIDDLE　　　　HIGH

읽는 시간(Reading time)

7분 46초
LOW　　　　MIDDLE　　　　HIGH

말하는 시간(Speaking Time)
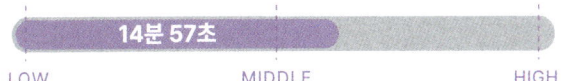
14분 57초
LOW　　　　MIDDLE　　　　HIGH

LEVEL 3

Chapter 1

The Fireplace Maid

There once was a girl named Ella. She was so gentle and beautiful that everyone loved her. When she was young, her mother died.

Her stepmother wanted to give everything to her own daughters, not Ella. She gave good clothes to her daughters, but Ella had only old clothes. They were the only ones who didn't love her. She worked in the kitchen and sat by the fireplace. Her sisters didn't do anything all day; they just sat on chairs.

Now the King and Queen had only one son. They were worried about finding him a wife, so they decided to invite all the finest ladies to a party. They hoped the Prince could choose his wife among them.

Cinderella's stepmother and her stepsisters were invited. They were very excited because they hoped the Prince would choose them. Her sisters watched him from the windows, and he was so cheerful and gentle. Every lady wanted to marry him. The sisters bought all the finest clothes. They got great jewels, feathers for their hair, and shiny fans for themselves. Her stepmother's dress was beautiful as well.

Cinderella sighed and said, "I wish I could go to the party too. I want to see that handsome Prince."
"You!" shouted the sisters, laughing. "You would look ridiculous at the party. Go wash the pots and pans," shouted her stepmother. "That's all you can do,

you cinder-wench." So Cinderella went back to her work, but as she cleaned and cleaned, she cried a lot. She could not see through her tears.

Chapter 2
The Fairy's Gift

On the night of the party, the sisters wore wonderful dresses and jewels. They went to the kitchen to show them to Cinderella, wanting to make her jealous. They smiled and looked at her as her stepmother got on the carriage to go to the party. While sitting by the fire, Cinderella cried and cried.

Suddenly, an old woman in a hat appeared in the kitchen. Nobody knew where she came from. Her eyes shone

and twinkled like two stars, and she carried a magic wand in her hand. Cinderella was surprised and looked at her.

"Why are you crying, my child?" the old woman asked. Cinderella wondered who she was and answered, "I am so sad that I cannot go to the party. I want to go there like my sisters."

"You don't need to cry," said the fairy godmother, "I know you are a good girl. Please do as I say, and you can have anything you wish. Run to the garden and bring me a pumpkin; if there are six fine mice, they will be useful."

Cinderella went to the garden and found a mousetrap with six mice in it. She also found a big, round pumpkin. She carried them to the fairy godmother.

"That is good," she said. "We are ready to begin now." After the fairy godmother touched the pumpkin with her magic wand, it turned into a great carriage. The six mice became six gray horses, and a rat in the trap turned into a horseman. He got up on the carriage, held the lines, and sat there, waiting.

Suddenly, the fairy godmother yelled, "Servants! Servants!" She started looking for something to use as servants. She found two lizards in a crack in the wall and, with her magic wand, transformed them into servants. One wore a wig, and the other wore a hat. "All is ready! This is the best carriage!" said the fairy godmother.

"Wait! I can't go in my old clothes," cried Cinderella. Her old clothes weren't suitable for the party. The fairy godmother touched her clothes, and they began changing into a fantastic dress. Diamonds sparkled in her hair, and delicate glass shoes fit her perfectly.

Cinderella was overjoyed. Her dress and diamonds twinkled brightly. "You can go to the party," said the fairy godmother, "But you must come home by 12 o'clock. If you don't, everything will turn back—your dress, carriage, and servants will change again." Cinderella promised to listen to her, and then she got on the carriage.

Chapter 3

The First Ball

Finally, Cinderella could see the castle. The Prince was looking for a lady to dance with. All the ladies were beautiful. They were all interested in him and waited for him.

Just then, Cinderella appeared in the room. Everyone looked at her because she was the most beautiful of them all. As soon as the Prince saw her, he approached. "Could you be my partner? You are the most beautiful lady I have ever seen." He fell in love with Cinderella.

They began dancing together. All the ladies thought she deserved it because she was so pretty. The Prince wondered where she came from, but he couldn't even find out her name.

It was fifteen minutes before midnight when Cinderella suddenly disappeared from the room, boarded the carriage, and headed home. The Prince didn't know who she was.

After she returned home, she sat by the fire. Her stepsisters also arrived.
"How was it?" she asked.
"It was a great party," they replied.
"Who did the Prince choose?"
"A mysterious princess arrived later, and the Prince chose her. He seemed to fall in love with her. But the princess left the party before it ended, and

nobody knew where she came from. He is having another party tomorrow, hoping she will come back. He wants to meet her again."

Cinderella asked if she could join them.
"Please let me go with you. I really want to go to the party."
"Oh no," the sisters laughed.
"Going there with you would be too embarrassing for us. You are only a cinder-wench."

After that, the stepsisters went to bed because they had to attend the second party.

Chapter 4
The Second Ball

On the following night, the stepsisters prepared themselves and once again set off for the party. Cinderella wished to join them, even more than before.

After they left, the fairy godmother appeared in the kitchen. "I believe you also want to attend the party," she said. "I truly wish to," Cinderella answered.

The fairy godmother transformed a pumpkin, mice, a rat, and lizards into an elegant carriage, horses, a driver, and footmen. She also used her magic wand to turn Cinderella's old dress into a shining dress. With great joy, Cinderella entered the carriage and headed to the party.

As soon as she stepped into the room, the Prince quickly approached her and took her hand. "Why did you disappear so suddenly? I searched everywhere for you and missed you," he said. Then, he led her to dance with him again.

The night grew late, and Cinderella began to feel anxious. She had to leave before midnight, but the Prince continued to watch her closely. She finally asked him to let her go for just a moment, then ran down the stairs. She boarded the carriage and departed.

When the clock struck twelve o'clock, the magic began to fade. The carriage transformed back into a pumpkin, the

horses turned into mice, the horseman became a rat, and the lizards hid in a crack in the wall. Cinderella found herself in her old clothes again. She barely had time to rush back to the kitchen.

She stood by the fire just before the door opened and her sisters entered. "This party was even more charming than the previous one," they exclaimed. "And the Princess was there again! She looked so lovely, and the Prince had eyes only for her."

"Oh, if only I could catch a glimpse of her!" sighed Cinderella.

"You, the cinder-wench!" the sisters ridiculed. "She wouldn't even let you in her kitchen. Now help us change out of our dresses. There's another party tomorrow, and we have to rest."

Cinderella assisted her stepsisters in removing their dresses. While doing so, they spoke repeatedly about the unknown princess, how beautiful she was, and how the Prince admired her.

Chapter 5
The Midnight Escape

On the following night, Cinderella assisted her sisters in dressing for the party. They departed in a large carriage, while Cinderella waited for her fairy godmother to arrive. Before long, the kind, elderly fairy godmother appeared.

"Well," she said, "do you also want to go to this party?"

"Oh, dear Godmother!" exclaimed Cinderella. "I wish to go more than I've ever wished for anything in my entire life."

"Very well, then you shall go," replied the fairy godmother. "But remember, you must leave before the clock strikes twelve. If you don't, your fine dress will turn into old rags, and your sisters will recognize you."

Cinderella promised, and her godmother then touched her with the magic wand. The dirty rags covering Cinderella transformed into an even more perfect dress than before, and she looked more gorgeous, her beauty shining like the full moon.

When she stepped into the party room, she was so charming that everyone found it hard to look away. The Prince couldn't stop staring at her and repeatedly asked who she was, but she would not answer. They danced together many times. Cinderella was so happy that she didn't notice the time slipping by.

Suddenly, the clock began to strike. Cinderella became frightened and let out a small cry. She quickly released the Prince's hand and ran away so fast that he couldn't catch up to her. She rushed down the stairs, accidentally dropping one of her little glass shoes along the way. There was no time to pick it up. She reached the door just as the clock sounded its last chime, and instantly her beautiful dress and glittering jewelry vanished. She stood there once again as a simple kitchen maid. Crying, she hurried back home.

She had no time to sit by the fire before her sisters returned. "Why are you crying?" they yelled. "What do you have to cry about? You sit here comfortably with no reason to be sad! The party tonight was amazing! The Princess was unbelievably beautiful, and the Prince only looked at her. Still, she left again, and we don't know where she went. The Prince found only her glass shoe on the stairs. Maybe he can find her using it."

Chapter 6
The Glass Slipper

The following day, the Prince announced that he had found the glass shoe and would find his bride with it. He missed her so much and hoped to be reunited. The messenger brought the shoe to many houses, allowing every lady a chance to try it on. However, it fit no one.

At last, the messenger arrived at Cinderella's house. The stepsisters were quite excited and tried on the special shoe. One sister couldn't fit her foot in, and the other failed as well. Their mother insisted they try again, but the messenger asked, "Is there anyone else in this house?"

He had to check every lady in the city. Finally, the stepmother called for Cinderella. Cinderella came right away, looking so sweet.

The messenger was puzzled that she was just a girl from the kitchen. She sat and took the shoe from him, and it fit perfectly. Then she withdrew the matching shoe from under her old clothes. The messenger realized that she was the mysterious princess the Prince had chosen. He knelt and said, "You are the princess the Prince has been searching for."

The stepmother and stepsisters were deeply angry and envious. They wanted to send Cinderella back to the kitchen, but the messenger stopped them. He took her to the palace and dressed her in fine clothing of a princess.

When the Prince saw her again, his heart overflowed with love and joy. Soon, they held their wedding. The sisters and mother did not attend; they were too embarrassed and furious. However, the Prince and Cinderella lived together happily ever after.

단계영어

신데렐라

LEVEL 4

단어(Words)

2205개
LOW　　　MIDDLE　　　HIGH

문장수(Sentences)
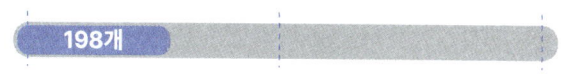
198개
LOW　　　MIDDLE　　　HIGH

문장길이(Sentence Length)

11.1
LOW　　　MIDDLE　　　HIGH

읽는 시간(Reading time)
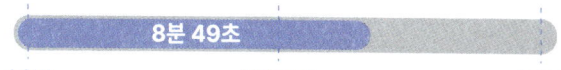
8분 49초
LOW　　　MIDDLE　　　HIGH

말하는 시간(Speaking Time)

16분 57초
LOW　　　MIDDLE　　　HIGH

LEVEL 4

Chapter 1
The Fireplace Maid

Once, there lived a girl named Cinderella. She was known for her gentleness and beauty; everyone who crossed her path loved her. She had a stepmother and stepsisters. They were expected to love her the most, but they did not. Her own mother passed away when she was young, and later her father remarried.

Her stepmother had two daughters of her own. She favored them, leaving Cinderella with nothing. The stepmother provided her daughters with fine dresses while leaving Cinderella to do household chores in the kitchen. She wore only worn-out clothes.

There was a fireplace in the kitchen with glowing embers, and she often sat near it for warmth. This was why her stepsisters called her "Cinder-Ella." (Cinder means the dust or small pieces left from burned wood.)

The King and Queen had an only son, and they worried about his marriage since he had yet to find his bride. Eventually, they planned a grand dance party, inviting the finest ladies in the land. They hoped the Prince might find his match among them.

All the important people were invited—including Cinderella's stepmother and stepsisters. The stepsisters were thrilled, eagerly watching the Prince from the windows. He was so cheerful and gentle that any woman would be lucky to marry him. The sisters received fine things to wear—satin, velvet, lace, jewels, feathers for their hair, and shiny fans. The stepmother's dress was also elegant.

Cinderella sighed deeply. "I wish I could go to the dance party and see the handsome Prince and the lovely ladies," she murmured. "You? You at the party? Look at your old clothes and sooty hands," the sisters shouted, laughing. "Go wash your pots and pans," the stepmother yelled. "That's all you're good for, you cinder-wench."

So, Cinderella returned to her work. As she scrubbed and wiped, tears streamed down her cheeks, clouding her vision.

Chapter 2
The Fairy's Gift

On the night of the party, Cinderella's sisters, adorned in dresses and jewels, paraded into the kitchen to show off. They moved around, displaying their dresses and smiling as they stole glances at her. Once they had their fill of compliments, they—along with the stepmother—departed for the party in a grand coach.

Amid her tears, a little old woman suddenly appeared in the kitchen. She wore a high-pointed hat and buckled shoes, and her origin was a mystery.

"Why are you crying so intensely?" the

woman inquired. Cinderella looked at her, wondering who she might be. "I'm crying because my sisters went to the party, and I wanted to go too."

"No need to cry," said the elderly woman reassuringly. "Don't worry. I am your fairy godmother. Listen carefully and follow my instructions. If you do as I say, nothing will be important for you. Go to the garden and fetch me a pumpkin. Also, bring the mousetrap—the six mice inside will be of use."

Just as she instructed, Cinderella found six mice in the mousetrap and brought the biggest, roundest pumpkin from the garden. "Excellent," remarked the godmother. Then, she turned the pumpkin into a magnificent coach with yellow satin, and the mice transformed into six handsome, glossy gray horses. The rat from the trap became a coachman adorned with gold lace. He climbed onto the coach, took the reins, and sat there holding them.

"Servants! Servants!" the godmother urgently called. "Where can we find them?" She looked around and noticed two lizards. With a wave of her wand, they transformed into servants with powdered wigs and detailed hats. They stood behind the coach. "And now," the fairy stated, "everything is prepared. This is the most magnificent coach for the party. Don't you agree?"

"Godmother, my dress! No matter how magnificent the coach is, I can't go to the party in my old clothes," Cinderella exclaimed.

"Wait! I have something." The godmother touched Cinderella's ragged clothes with her wand, and instantly they turned into a blue satin dress adorned with pearls. Diamonds adorned her hair, and her clumsy shoes transformed into glass slippers that perfectly fit her small feet.

Cinderella was both shocked and incredibly delighted. The satin of her dress gleamed like the moon, and the diamonds in her hair shimmered like her stars.

"Now, you can attend the party," the godmother announced. "But remember this: My magic will only last until midnight. At the stroke of twelve, your fine clothes will revert to old clothes; the coach will become a pumpkin again, the horses will turn into mice, and the coachman and servants will transform back into a rat and lizards, just as they were before. You must return home by twelve."

Cinderella promised to pay attention to the warning, then climbed into the coach and set off for the party.

Chapter 3
The First Ball

Upon arriving at the palace, Cinderella was greeted by music. All the ladies awaited the Prince, as he was about to select a partner for the dance. Each lady wished to be chosen by him. Determining the most beautiful was no easy task.

However, when Cinderella entered the room, all eyes were drawn to her. She radiated beauty akin to the moon's glow. The Prince approached her and extended his hand. "You will be my dance partner," he declared. "I have never encountered anyone as beautiful as you." He inquired about her name and origin, but she declined to reveal them.

Just as the castle clock chimed a quarter to twelve, she slipped away to her coach; the rat coachman cracked his whip, and they sped away, leaving the Prince unaware of her departure.

When her stepsisters returned home, Cinderella sat by the fire, once again dressed in old clothes. "Was the party enjoyable?" she inquired. "Yes, it was indeed a splendid party," the sisters responded. "Who danced with the Prince?" Cinderella asked. "He danced with a mysterious princess who arrived later," they replied. "Initially, the Prince was amiable toward us, flashing smiles. He could have chosen one of us as his dance partner. However, the moment the mysterious princess appeared, he couldn't take his eyes off her. She must be a princess of great importance, for no one could identify her—not even the Prince, despite his pleas for her to reveal herself. Before the party finished, she vanished, leaving everyone puzzled. The Prince was quite concerned and perplexed. He is hosting another party tomorrow night, hoping that the princess will return so he can uncover her identity."

Cinderella let out a saddened sigh. "Please, allow me to go with you tomorrow. Just lend me an old dress. That will suffice."

"What are you saying?" her stepsisters

laughed mockingly. "You? A wretched girl like you? It would be insulting for us to be seen with you. We'd be mortified if anyone noticed us together. The kitchen is your rightful place."

They then ordered her to take off their dresses. "We need rest for the second party," they stated before retiring for the night.

Chapter 4
The Second Ball

The following night, the stepsisters got ready and headed to the party, deepening Cinderella's longing to join them. As soon as they departed, the fairy godmother appeared in the kitchen again. "Well," she began, "I suppose you also want to attend the party." "Oh, dear Fairy Godmother, I truly wish I could!" Cinderella exclaimed.

The fairy godmother requested a pumpkin, mice, a rat, and lizards. With her magic, she transformed them into an elegant coach, horses, a driver, and footmen. Then, with a wave of her wand, Cinderella's old dress became a beautiful gown—even lovelier than the one she had worn the night before.

Happily, Cinderella stepped into the coach and journeyed to the party. The Prince had been eagerly awaiting her appearance.

As soon as she entered the room, he rushed to greet her, taking her hand. "Why did you leave without saying goodbye?" he asked. "I searched everywhere for you and couldn't sleep all night." He led her onto the dance floor again, focusing on her alone.

As midnight neared, Cinderella felt a surge of anxiety. The Prince continued following her intently, so she cleverly excused herself for a moment and quickly departed. She put on her cloak, hurried down the stairs, and boarded her waiting coach, which sped away. But as she traveled, the castle clock started to strike. When the chimes faded, her coach changed into a pumpkin, the horses back into mice, the driver into a rat, and the lizards into their normal selves, hiding in the walls.

Dressed again in her old and torn clothes, Cinderella hurried back to the kitchen, standing by the fire as her stepsisters came in.

"This party was even more enchanting than the last," they said. "That Princess appeared again, shining like a star. The

Prince was focused solely on her."

"Oh, if only I could see her!" Cinderella sighed. "You, the girl who deals with cinders!" they mocked. "She wouldn't let you in her own kitchen. Never mind that—help us change out of our dresses. There's another party tomorrow, and we want to look perfect."

Cinderella assisted them, listening to their endless talk of the mysterious princess whose beauty seemed to captivate the Prince.

Chapter 5

The Midnight Escape

The following night, Cinderella helped her sisters dress and get ready for the party. They departed in their elegant coach, and Cinderella eagerly awaited her godmother's arrival.

The elderly fairy soon appeared. "Well," she said, "do you wish to go to this party as well?" "Oh, dear Godmother!" Cinderella exclaimed. "I want to go more than anything I've ever wanted in my life."

"All right, then you shall go," said the godmother. "But remember, you must leave before the clock strikes twelve. If you don't, your gorgeous clothes will turn into rags in front of everyone, and your sisters will see that you're the cinder girl."

Cinderella promised. Her godmother then tapped her with the magic wand, and in a flash, her shabby clothes changed into the most dazzling gown yet. She looked more stunning than ever, appearing as radiant as the full moon.

When she entered the party room, all eyes fell on her. The Prince couldn't look away and constantly asked who she was, but she refused to say. They danced together numerous times, and Cinderella was so overjoyed that she lost track of time.

Suddenly, the clock began to chime, and Cinderella was startled. She let go of the Prince's hand and dashed away. He couldn't keep up with her. Rushing down the stairs, she accidentally dropped one of her glass slippers but was too frightened and hurried to pick it up.

By the time she reached the door, the last of the twelve chimes ended, and her glamorous attire disappeared. Her jewels vanished, and the guard watching the door merely saw a distressed kitchen girl passing by, her face streaked with tears.

Cinderella returned home as swiftly as possible, managing to sit by the fire before her sisters arrived. "Why are you crying so much?" they asked. "You're safe and warm. But listen, the party tonight was more incredible than we expected! That mysterious Princess was more beautiful than ever, and the Prince couldn't look at anyone but her. She disappeared again and left a single slipper on the stairs. Maybe the Prince will find her with it!"

Chapter 6
The Glass Slipper

The next day, the Prince made a big announcement. He had found a special glass slipper, and whoever could wear it would become his bride. Although the princess had run away from him three times, he still wished to find her and asked his messenger to visit every household, letting each lady try on the shoe.

Everyone was certain they could wear it, but no one could. Some had feet that were too long, others too wide, and others too large or too small.

Finally, the messenger arrived at Cinderella's home. The stepsisters were thrilled. They each tried the shoe, but it didn't fit either of them. One sister couldn't get her heel in, and the other couldn't even push her toes inside.

The mother urged them to try again, but the messenger said, "Is there anyone else in this house who might wear the slipper?" Since the sisters failed, the mother insisted that nobody else mattered. Still, the messenger was under orders to let everyone try. The stepmother reluctantly called for Cinderella, and she appeared immediately, looking modest yet lovely.

Surprised to see she was only the kitchen maid, the messenger still had her sit and try on the shoe. She slipped it on perfectly. Then, she pulled the other glass slipper out from under her ragged clothes and put it on her other foot. The messenger instantly knew she was the mysterious princess. He knelt before her and said, "You are the lady the Prince has chosen."

The stepmother and stepsisters grew furious and jealous, wanting to send Cinderella back to the kitchen. But the messenger refused, taking Cinderella instead to the palace.

There, she was dressed like a true princess.

When the Prince saw her again, radiant and graceful, he felt overwhelming love and joy. They were wed soon thereafter, though the stepsisters were too ashamed to attend. The stepmother felt bitter, and her anger made her unwell. Meanwhile, the Prince and Cinderella lived happily ever after.

단계영어

· 신데렐라 ·

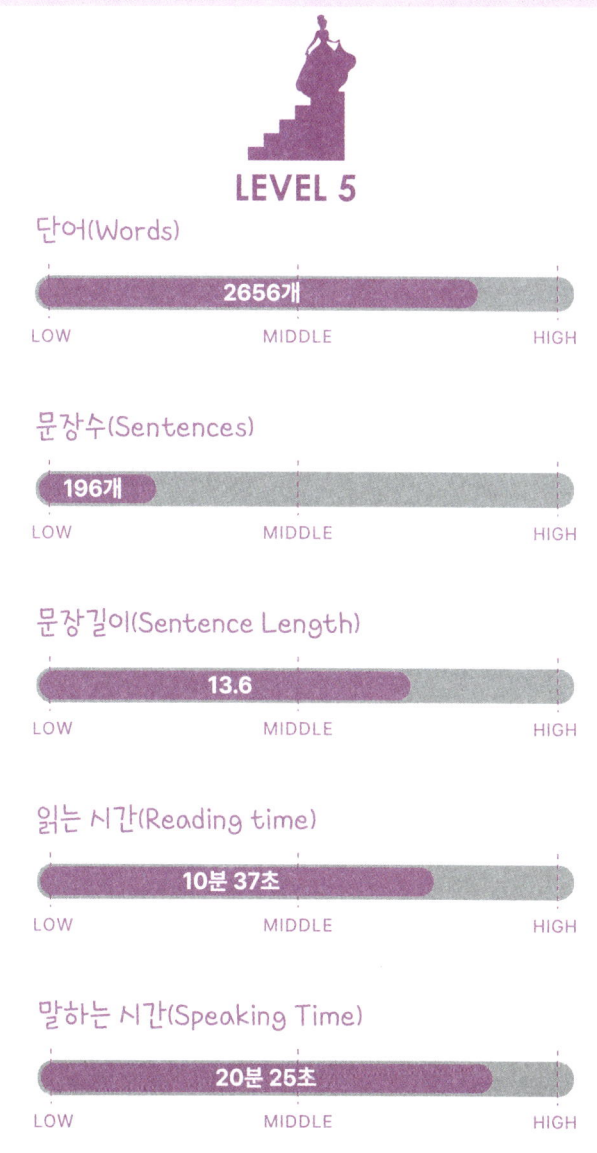

LEVEL 5

단어(Words)
2656개
LOW　　　　　　MIDDLE　　　　　　HIGH

문장수(Sentences)
196개
LOW　　　　　　MIDDLE　　　　　　HIGH

문장길이(Sentence Length)
13.6
LOW　　　　　　MIDDLE　　　　　　HIGH

읽는 시간(Reading time)
10분 37초
LOW　　　　　　MIDDLE　　　　　　HIGH

말하는 시간(Speaking Time)
20분 25초
LOW　　　　　　MIDDLE　　　　　　HIGH

THE
ORIGINAL
TEXT

Chapter 1
The Fireplace Maid

There was once a girl named Ella who was so gentle and beautiful that everyone who knew her loved her—except those who should have loved her best, and those were her stepmother and her stepsisters. Her own mother had died while she was quite young, and then her father had married again.

This new wife had two daughters of her own, and she wished them to have everything while Ella had nothing. The stepmother dressed her own children in fine clothes, and they sat about and did nothing all day, but Cinderella worked in the kitchen with only rags to wear. Because she often sat close to the ashes to warm herself, her sisters called her Cinderella.

Now, the King and Queen of that country had only one son, and they were very anxious for him to marry, but he had never seen anyone he wished to make his bride.

At last, they decided to give a great ball and invite all the fairest ladies in the land, hoping that among them all the Prince might find someone to choose. All the grand people of the city were invited, including Cinderella's stepmother and her stepsisters.

The stepsisters were extremely excited; both of them were so certain of their own beauty that they hoped the Prince might choose one of them. They had often watched him ride by, so gay and gallant that anyone might have been glad to marry him.

All sorts of fine things were bought for the sisters to wear—satins, velvets, laces, jewels, feathers for their hair, and glittering fans to carry. Their mother's dress was no less fine than theirs.

Cinderella sighed and sighed. "I wish I might go to the ball, too, and see that handsome Prince and all the lovely ladies," she said.

"You!" cried the sisters, laughing. "A pretty sight you would be at the ball, you with your rags and your sooty hands."

"Go scour your pots and pans," cried the stepmother. "That's all you're fit for, you cinder-wench."

So Cinderella went back to her work. As she scrubbed and rubbed, tears ran so fast down her cheeks that she could hardly see.

Chapter 2
The Fairy's Gift

On the night of the ball the sisters dressed themselves in all their finery and came into the kitchen to show themselves to Cinderella.

They hoped to make her envious. They swept up and down the room, spreading their gowns, smiling and eyeing themselves while Cinderella looked on admiringly.

After they tired of her admiration, the sisters and the stepmother stepped into a fine coach and went gaily away to the ball. But Cinderella sat in a corner by the fire and wept bitterly.

Suddenly, while she wept, a little old woman in a high-pointed hat and buckled shoes appeared in the kitchen, and no one could have told where she came from. Her eyes shone and twinkled like two stars, and she carried a wand in her hand.

"Why are you so sad, my child?" she asked. "Why do you weep so bitterly?"

Cinderella looked at her in wonder. "I am weeping," she said, "because my sisters have gone to the ball without me, and I, too, wished I could have gone."

"Then dry your tears," said the little old woman. "I am your fairy godmother. If you are a good girl and do exactly as I say, there is nothing you can wish for that you shall not have. Run to the garden and fetch me a pumpkin, and let me see the mousetrap. If there are six fine, fat mice in it, they will be of use."

Cinderella did as she was told. She found exactly six mice in the trap and hurried out to the garden to fetch the biggest, roundest pumpkin she could find.

"That is well," said the godmother. "And now the

rattrap." Cinderella brought it, and indeed there was a rat in it. "Now we are ready to begin."

She touched the pumpkin with her wand, and at once it turned into a magnificent golden coach lined throughout with pale yellow satin. She touched the mice, and they became six handsome, sleek gray horses to draw the coach. She touched the rat, and he was turned into a coachman in a livery of scarlet and gold lace. He mounted the box of the coach, gathered up the reins, and waited, whip in hand.

"Footmen! Footmen!" cried the godmother impatiently. "Where shall we get them?" Her sharp eyes glanced this way and that, and presently in a crack of the wall she saw two lizards.

"The very thing," she said. A touch of her wand changed them into footmen with powdered wigs and cocked hats. They sprang up and took their places behind the coach.

"And now," cried the fairy, "all is ready, and no one has a finer coach. Don't you agree?"

"But, Godmother, my rags! I could never go to the ball in these, no matter how fine the coach," cried Cinderella.

"Wait a bit! I have not finished yet." With that, the godmother touched Cinderella's rags with her wand, and they transformed into a gown of blue satin embroidered with pearls. Diamonds sparkled in her hair, and her rough shoes became glass slippers that fit her little feet exactly.

Cinderella could hardly believe her eyes, and her heart was filled with joy. The satin gleamed around her like moonshine, and the diamonds were as bright as the tears she had shed.

"Now, my child, you can go to the ball," said the godmother. "But remember: my fairy charm can only last until twelve o'clock. At the last stroke of twelve, these fine clothes will change back into rags; the coach will again become a pumpkin, the horses will turn into mice, and the coachman and the footmen will become a rat and lizards as they were before. So you must be home by twelve."

Cinderella promised to obey and then stepped into the coach and rolled away to the ball.

Chapter 3
The First Ball

When she reached the palace, music was playing and the Prince was about to choose a partner for the dance.

All the ladies stood by, waiting anxiously, each hoping to be the one he chose. Many beauties were present, and it was hard to say who was the loveliest. But when Cinderella entered the room, no one looked at anyone else. She was far more fair than the fairest, as the crescent moon outshines the stars.

The Prince came directly to her and took her by the hand. "You shall be my partner in the dance," said he, "for never have I seen anyone so fair."

From then on he danced with no one but Cinderella, and not one person blamed him, for her beauty melted every heart. The Prince begged her to tell him her name and where she came from, but she would not.

At the quarter before twelve, the castle clock gave a warning chime, and Cinderella managed to slip away from him and run out to her coach. She sprang in, the rat coachman cracked his whip, and away they went. The Prince did not even see her go.

When the stepsisters returned home, Cinderella was again sitting by the fire in her rags. "Was it a beautiful ball?" she asked.

"Yes, indeed it was," they answered, and they eagerly told her of every detail.

"And whom did the Prince dance with?" asked Cinderella.

"Oh, he danced with a strange princess who came in after the ball began. At first, the Prince bowed to us and smiled, and he might have chosen one of us, but once he saw her, he had eyes for no other. She must be a very great princess indeed, though no one could say who she was, not even the Prince. He begged her to tell him, but she slipped away before the ball was over, and no one knew where she'd gone. The Prince was in despair. He's giving another ball tomorrow night, hoping she will return, and then perhaps he will find out who she is."

Cinderella sighed. "Oh, dear sisters, let me go with you tomorrow, I beg of you. One of your old dresses would do for me."

But the sisters only laughed. "You, the cinder-wench! No, no—the kitchen is the place for you. We would die of shame if anyone saw you among those fine folk." With that they had Cinderella unfasten their dresses and help them to bed so they'd be fresh for the next evening's ball.

Chapter 4
The Second Ball

The following night the stepsisters dressed again for the ball, and they drove away while Cinderella longed more than ever to go with them. Hardly had they left when the fairy godmother again appeared in the kitchen.

"Well," she asked, "would you like to go to this ball, too?"

"Oh, dear Godmother, if I only could!" cried Cinderella.

The godmother asked for a pumpkin, the mice, the rat, and the lizards, just as before. She transformed them into a grand coach, horses, a driver, and footmen. Then she touched Cinderella's rags with her wand, changing them into a dress even more dazzling than the night before. Thus arrayed, Cinderella stepped into the coach and rolled away to the ball.

The Prince had been on the lookout for her, and the moment she entered the room, he hurried to her and took her by the hand.

"Why did you leave me so suddenly?" he asked. "I searched everywhere and could not sleep all night for thinking of you." He again led her to dance, and once more he devoted himself to no one else.

As midnight neared, Cinderella felt uneasy. She tried to slip away unnoticed, but the Prince followed her closely. At last, she made some quick excuse and left him. She drew her cloak about her, hurried down the stairs, and boarded her waiting coach.

Partway home, she heard the clock begin to chime. As the final stroke sounded, the coach melted from around her into a yellow pumpkin. The horses became mice and ran squeaking away, the coachman became a rat, and the lizards scurried into a crack. Dressed again in her rags, Cinderella just managed to run back to the kitchen and sit by the fire before the stepsisters arrived.

"The ball was even more wonderful than the one before," said the sisters. "And the Princess came again, so radiant it hurt the eyes to look at her. The Prince cared for no one else!"

"Ah, if only I could see her!" sighed Cinderella.

"You—see her, you cinder-wench?" mocked the sisters. "She wouldn't even let you in her kitchen. But never mind, help us off with our dresses. Tomorrow there is to be yet another ball, and we must rest to look our best." So Cinderella helped them undress while they talked endlessly about the beautiful princess and the admiration the Prince showed her.

Chapter 5

The Midnight Escape

On the third evening, Cinderella helped her sisters dress for the ball and watched them ride away. She waited impatiently for her godmother to come, which the old fairy soon did.

"Well," said the fairy, "do you wish to go to this ball, too?"

"Oh, dear Godmother!" Cinderella exclaimed. "I wish it more than I have ever wished for anything in my life."

"Then you shall go," said the fairy godmother. "But remember your promise: you must leave before the clock strikes twelve. If you do not, your fine clothes will become rags before them all, and your sisters will know you are truly the cinder-wench."

Cinderella promised. The fairy godmother touched her with the wand, turning her ragged clothes into an even more magnificent dress. If before she had seemed the crescent moon, now she shone like the full moon in all its glory.

As she entered the ballroom, she appeared so dazzling that people could scarcely look at her. The Prince followed her from place to place, begging her to tell him who she was, but she would not. They danced again and again, and Cinderella was so overjoyed she forgot to keep watch on the time.

Suddenly, the castle clock began to ring. Cinderella, terrified, snatched her hand away from the Prince and fled. She vanished so quickly that for a moment he lost sight of her. Such was her haste that she lost one of her little glass slippers on the stair but did not dare to stop and pick it up.

Just as she reached the door, the last stroke of twelve sounded. Her lovely gown turned back into

rags, and her jewels disappeared. The guard saw only a weary little kitchen girl run past, weeping bitterly.

Cinderella raced home as fast as her feet could carry her. She was just in time to seat herself by the fire before her stepsisters swept into the room.

"What! Still crying?" they asked. "What a silly little thing you are, to cry so much. You have a warm corner to sit in and no worries. Oh, but you should have seen tonight's ball! It outshone both the others, and the Princess was the most beautiful of all. The Prince did not so much as glance at anyone else, but she disappeared once more, and no one knows where. The Prince, however, found one of her slippers on the stairs, and perhaps he can find her by that."

Chapter 6
The Glass Slipper

The next day, the Prince made a proclamation far and wide: he had found a glass slipper, and whoever could wear it should become his bride. He hoped in this way to find the lovely Princess who had eluded him thrice.

The slipper was carried from one house to another, and every lady was eager to try it on. One after another, they failed—some had feet too long, some too broad, some too fat, and some too thin.

At last, the messenger came to Cinderella's house. The stepsisters could barely wait to try on the slipper; each was certain it would fit her. They quarreled over who would go first.

Finally, it was handed to the eldest sister, but though her toes slipped into it, her heel would not move down. Then the second sister tried, and she

could not even get her toes inside. The stepmother insisted they try again, but the messenger shook his head.

"No, no," he said. "Neither one is the right one. Is there no one else in this house who might try it on?"

No, there was only the little kitchen maid. If the daughters could not wear it, she certainly could not. Still, the messenger said he must see her, for his orders were that every woman in the city try the slipper.

Reluctantly, the stepmother called for Cinderella. She came at once, looking so modest and so lovely that the messenger wondered how she came to be only a kitchen-wench. She sat down, took the slipper, and put it on; it fit exactly. Then she drew out the other slipper from beneath her rags and put it on her other foot.

Instantly, the messenger knew she must be the one the Prince was seeking. He knelt before her.

"You, my lady, are the bride the Prince has chosen," he said.

The stepmother and stepsisters were wild with envy and anger. They could hardly believe their eyes and would have sent Cinderella back to the kitchen if the messenger had not prevented them.

Cinderella was taken to the palace and dressed as a princess should be. When the Prince saw her so beautiful, his heart overflowed with love and joy.

Soon they were married, and though the stepsisters were invited to the wedding, they were too ashamed to appear; their faces were still mottled from weeping. As for the stepmother, she was quite ill from rage and spite. But the Prince and Cinderella lived happily forever after.